THE COLLEGE SELECTION WORKBOOK

Cover Design: Roni Mocan
Cover Illustration: Ed Koren
Illustrations: Brian Bair

Published in the United States by
Beckham Publications Group, Inc.
P.O. Box 4066, Silver Spring, MD 20914

ISBN: 093176120-4

1   0   9   8   7   6   5   4   3   2   1

THE COLLEGE SELECTION WORKBOOK

Self-Paced Exercises to Help
You Choose the Right College

Third Edition

Barry Beckham

THE Beckham
PUBLICATIONS GROUP, INC

ACKNOWLEDGEMENTS

I first want to thank Linda Mahdesian, a Brown University undergraduate at the time for suggesting the idea of a workbook for high school students. She actually prepared the first draft about twenty years ago.

Also, I thank Dr. Mark Fisher, president of Fisher Educational Consultants in Atlanta, Georgia for his valuable suggestions for improvement so generously offered.

Finally, I think the many high school guidance counselors who have encouraged the continued updating of the workbook.

August, 2005

CONTENTS

THE VALUE OF A COLLEGE EDUCATION

When you decide that college is for you, you will have made a decision about an experience that will affect you in many ways.

First, of course, you will grow intellectually, opening your mind to the best that has been thought and written. You will learn how to reason, and to improve your skills in both verbal and written expression.

Through interaction with students with different perspectives, from different socio-economic levels and from different parts of the country, you will grow socially as well as emotionally.

The skills you develop as a college student will prepare you to take advantage of opportunities that non-college graduates can only dream about. For example, the U.S. Census Bureau reports that for college graduates the average yearly income is 45% higher than that of someone with only a high school diploma. In a lifetime, the college graduate earns 1.8 times the amount that a high school graduate makes.

Translated, that means if a high school graduate can make $14,000 per year, the college graduate will make almost $21,000. If the high school graduate's lifetime earnings amount to $500,000, the college graduate's will total nearly $730,000.

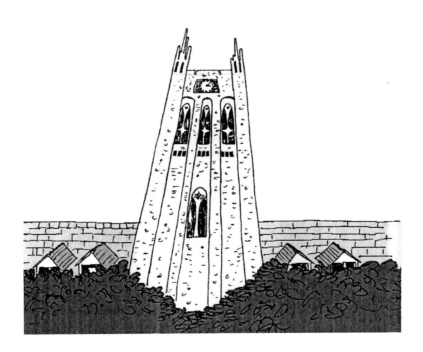

IS COLLEGE FOR ME?

It's not for everybody. For some, college is neither necessary nor valuable. It really depends on your goals in life. The first part of this book helps you look at who you are and what you want.

First, you should look at your occupational interests. Is a four-year degree mandatory? Yes, if you want to be an attorney, physician or teacher. No, if you are interested in medical assisting, bookkeeping or a trade and a host of other occupations that don't demand a four-year degree. Perhaps, a two-year associate degree would be more appropriate.

Consider what you want to do, what your goals are.

Secondly, think about the discipline and intellectual challenges you'll have to handle. Are you really ready?

A very important part of the college selection process is looking at yourself. The colleges you select to apply to should reflect your career goals, your academic profile, your interests, your personality, and your values. You should not select a list of colleges to apply to until you know who you are.

This workbook should make the selection process easier for you. Yes, you will have to put in time and do a little homework, but when you are making a decision valued at over $100,000 in some cases, it is well worth the time and energy you put into the process. Or you could choose a college based on how good their logo looks on a sweatshirt, like the student on the book cover.

WHY THE SELF-PACED METHOD?

The self-paced method of choosing a college is a sound approach because it is controlled by you. It's your future, so why shouldn't you be in charge?

In the profound American novel, *Invisible Man*, by Ralph Ellison, the narrator says that all his life he had allowed others to determine the direction of his life when in fact nobody could define him better than he could himself.

The best time to start this self-evaluation is no later than the beginning of your junior year in high school. You could start earlier or later. However, in your junior year, you will have a good idea where your grade point average (GPA) falls and what your PSAT, SAT or ACT scores are.

The rate at which you proceed is determined by you—just as you will be responsible for every decision you make for the rest of your life.

The self-paced method is therefore a good introduction to the in-charge-of-yourself philosophy you will need to be a successful undergraduate at the college of your choice.

The self-paced method reminds you that you need to follow a plan in a systematic manner to achieve your goals.

We have set up several inventories and exercises. As you complete the various tasks, you will learn important things about yourself, related to your educational future.

Take your time and answer honestly. Remember, the more you know about your needs, interests, goals and priorities, the better equipped you will be to select a college that is a proper match for you.

Although you should complete the tasks yourself, you should discuss your responses with your family. Others may have insights that can help you make decisions. Often, by discussing these matters with others, you hear them out, listen to their views and then make your decision.

These exercises will take time to complete. However, when you are making such an investment of as many as four years and thousands of dollars, the time you put into these exercises will be well worth the effort. It is only your future we are talking about. Is that important to you? We hope you answered with a resounding yes.

How Long Should It Take?

It depends.

You probably can't spend too much time and can't start too early. But you can definitely start too late and spend too little time.

Enterprising sophomores and juniors may spend a year or two carefully working through the exercises, as they think about the most important decision they will have made at this point in their lives.

Others will rush through the questions and answer them all in the fall of their senior year.

Ideally, the entire senior year should be devoted to the systematic evaluating of yourself and the colleges. The junior year, or at least half of it, could be spent getting acquainted with the colleges before you begin the serious sizing-up of your options.

To use this workbook effectively, set deadlines for yourself. Make a schedule of target dates to have each activity completed and stick to it. After all in college you will have to schedule your time effectively.

WHO CAN HELP ME?

As many people as you can find, who have valuable advice, can help you in this process. You will sense how useful their advice is by asking if it gives you a better understanding of the process.

Traditionally, your search begins with your guidance counselor. Your counselor can tell you about the strengths and weaknesses of some institutions and may have contacts at many.

You should contact the college admission office for information on entrance requirements and scholarship information.

Currently enrolled undergraduates can give you valuable information about a process they've already experienced.

Don't forget your teachers.

Other high school students may be especially knowledgeable about a particular school or a particular part of the application process. And they could be getting advice from an older brother or sister who is already in college.

Your parents will of course have some input.

Try also to find some recent graduates of colleges who can share with you the benefit of their mistakes as well as successes.

Several Internet sites also offer information about colleges, career counseling, and placement.

In short, you want to get as much useful advice as you can, as long as you remember the adage that free advice is usually worth what you pay for it.

TYPES OF EDUCATIONAL INSTITUTIONS

There are a variety of ways to prepare for your future after high school.

Look at all the options to be sure that college is—or is not—the best alternative for you.

Here is the range of possibilities you should consider.

OCCUPATIONAL TRAINING

Certain industries offer programs that combine classroom and on-the-job supervised training in a variety of skilled trades. Often accomplished through apprenticeships, you have the opportunity to earn as you learn while also studying under a master craftsperson. Programs may last from one to six years.

CAREER ACADEMIES

Career academies offer training, and often certification, in specific technical careers. These often include fields like drafting and allied medical fields.

BUSINESS SCHOOLS

You can pursue training relevant to office skills, business management and business administration. Programs usually range from 12 to 18 months.

TECHNICAL INSTITUTES

These offer programs, usually two or three years in length, for entry into highly technical trades. You will want to investigate this option if you wish to pursue a career as a medical technician, culinary artist, computer programmer or electronic technician. Entry requirements will normally include a high-school diploma, often including specific courses, but may also include several years of college work.

JUNIOR/COMMUNITY COLLEGES

Two-year programs can lead to an associate degree in a wide variety of programs. These can either enrich your education or help you prepare for semi-professional occupations. You would pursue an associate degree if you do not plan to continue your education past two years, but you can enter the associate degree college transfer program if you decide to continue on for a four-year bachelor's degree.

ENLISTMENT IN THE ARMED SERVICES

Several opportunities are available through enrollment in the armed services. You often have the opportunity to gain free technical training, often on advanced equipment, and many branches will actively encourage you to academically upgrade. In addition to this training, opportunities exist to develop a college fund during enlistment.

UNITED STATES ACADEMIES

Candidates to become officers in the Air Force, Army, Coast Guard, Marines, Merchant Marine and Navy are trained and educated at these academies expense-free. Following the completion of studies, a period of service in the branch may be required.

Engineering and liberal arts are combined in these four-year college programs. You should be aware that entry into these institutions is highly competitive and by Congressional appointment. You should begin applying for these academies in the spring of your junior year.

MILITARY INSTITUTES AND COLLEGES

Similar in program to the direct military academies, these are either state-sponsored or private schools. Commissioning into the armed services is generally optional.

LIBERAL ARTS COLLEGES

These offer four-year programs that focus the student into one field (a "major") during the last two years. These "majors" can include fields like physics, French, literature or economics, and some colleges even offer majors in pre-professional studies for fields like law and medicine. In addition to your major, you may often pursue a lesser concentration (a "minor") in a second field. This means that you could major in economics and minor in English.

UNIVERSITIES

Universities are congregations of more than one school or colleges. You will likely find schools of agriculture, business administration, education, engineering, journalism, law, arts, liberal arts, medicine, and nursing. These institutions also offer post-graduate degrees in several disciplines.

OTHER OPPORTUNITIES

Going off to college may not be the best option for you. Perhaps you want to work or pursue some alternative goals for a while. Does this mean that your opportunities for post-secondary education are finished for the time being? Absolutely not. There are a number of other opportunities to carry on your education outside of the formal college or university setting.

CORRESPONDENCE PROGRAMS

Many colleges and universities offer correspondence programs, usually through their part-time and continuing education departments. These courses are offered to people that cannot travel to the classroom. The instructor mails out the course lesson and assignment complete with deadline. You complete the assignments and mail them back to the instructor. These are generally fully accredited courses and can be counted toward a diploma or a degree. You can check out a wide variety of these organizations through The Distance Education and Training Council (www.detc.org), the Cook's Institute (www.cooks.edu), and the U.S. Guide to Distance Education.

ONLINE EDUCATION

The Internet has taken the correspondence course to the next level with on-line learning programs. Organizations like LearningChoices.com have begun to use the Internet as a means to run courses over the Internet, either on a fixed schedule or on demand. Prometheon (www.prometheon.com), eVisionInc (www.evisioninc.com), and the CSC (part of the Illinois Virtual Campus, www.ivc.illinois.edu/) all offer courses over the Internet. If you are looking for further information about online learning, take a quick look at the site at Butler Community College's web entitled "Is Online Learning for You?" (www.butlercc.edu/webcrs/about.cfm #Online)

If you are looking for the opportunity to learn as you earn, then cooperative education may be the answer for you. This arrangement combines the academic side of the classroom with the real-life work experience of employment in the field. The National Commission for Cooperative Education (www.co-op.edu) has been promoting cooperative education since 1962 and has numerous links to both schools and companies involved in this kind of learning. You can write for a guide to the following address: National Commission for Cooperative Education, 360 Huntington Avenue, Boston, MA 02115. The Cooperative Education Network (www.ocasppcp.uc.edu/home) also provides a page that will list the institutions subscribing to this form of education. Cooperative programs may take an additional year to complete; but it should be noted that you would leave with both an education and relevant experience.

CLEP

The College Level Examination Program (CLEP) allows students to earn credits by writing exams based on their life experience. You can get information about the CLEP at The College Board's CLEP for Students (www.collegeboard.com/student/testing/clep/about.html). If you have Adobe Acrobat, you can download the necessary forms at www.collegeboard.com/student/testing/clep/reg.html. This program can greatly assist you by lessening the number of credits you require for your degree or diploma.

ADVANCED PLACEMENT

There are several other similar ways to earn college credits, even while you are not attending college. Advanced placement will allow you to take a college level course as long as you meet the prerequisite requirements for the course. External placement will allow you to transfer credits between institutions. You can write for a guide to the American Council on Education, Publication Sales, Section 0061, Suite 30, One Dupont Circle, NW, Washington, DC 20036. Your employer may even offer to cover part or all of the costs of your education. Your college education need not be out of reach; you do have other options.

Introduction

You are about to make one of the most important decisions of your life. The college you attend will affect you psychologically, emotionally, physically, socially, and intellectually. You will spend the next four years of your life living and learning at that college. Now is the time to find out as much as you can about the college selection process.

Look Inside Yourself

But where do you start? You start by taking a good look at yourself: your interests, strengths, weaknesses and goals. This will help you focus in on what you want from a college.

We have set up a variety of inventories and exercises so that you can analyze the factors in the college admission process as they relate to you. As you complete the various tasks, you will learn about yourself as you prepare for the decisions that need to be made regarding your educational future.

Take your time and answer honestly. Remember, the more you know about your needs, interests, goals and priorities, the better equipped you will be to select a college that fits you.

While you should respond to the tasks on your own, you may and even should discuss your responses with your family. Others may have insights that can help you make decisions. Often, by discussing these matters with others, you hear them out, listen to their views, and then make your decision.

Use this selection process to learn about and evaluate yourself. Take your time and answer honestly. Remember, the more you know about your needs, interests, goals and priorities, the better equipped you will be to select a college that fits you.

These exercises will take time to complete. But when you are making an investment of thousands of dollars and anywhere from three to six years, the time you put into these exercises will be well worth the effort. It is only your future we are talking about. Is that important to you? We hope the answer is a resounding yes.

SELF INVENTORY CHART

I. Five Activities I enjoy (e.g. exercising, conducting chemistry experiments, singing, reading):

Activity	Why I Enjoy It

II. Six Strengths (e.g. analytical skills, athletic ability, public speaking, creativity):

III. Six Weaknesses (e.g. math ability, time management, lack of patience):

IV. My Top Five Careers or "If I Could Have Any Five Careers in the World, I Would Choose":

Career	Reasons Why

V. My Values and Needs (From the chart below, rank your needs and values from most important to least important. Number 1 is your most important and number 20 is your least important.):

Being emotionally secure	1.
Being famous for my work	2.
Being honest	3.
Being liked by my peers	4.
Being morally good	5.
Being rich	6.
Being the best in my field	7.
Experiencing love	8.
Getting graduate degree(s)	9.
Getting married	10.
Growing spiritually	11.
Having children	12.
Having financial security	13.
Helping others	14.
Leaving work at the office	15.
Living to work	16.
Maintaining good health	17.
Making positive social change	18.
Obtaining power	19.
Reaching my career goals	20.

MY PERSONAL ACADEMIC HISTORY

Use the charts below to help you evaluate your credentials and accomplishments that will be important in the college admission process. Fill in the blanks requiring information about grades, scores, rank and activities.

9th Grade

Subject	Grade	Test	Score	GPA/Class Rank	Awards and Honors
English		PSAT			
		1. Critical Reading			
		2. Math			
		3. Writing			
Math		SAT (current)			
		1. Math			
		2. Verbal			
		New SAT (class of 2006)			
		1. Critical Reading			
Science		2. Math			
		3. Writing			
		AP			
Social Studies		1.			
		2.			
		3.			

10th Grade

Subject	Grade	Test	Score	GPA/Class Rank	Awards and Honors
English		PSAT			
		4. Critical Reading			
		5. Math			
		6. Writing			
Math		SAT (current)			
		3. Math			
		4. Verbal			
		New SAT (class of 2006)			
		4. Critical Reading			
Science		5. Math			
		6. Writing			
		AP			
Social Studies		4.			
		5.			
		6.			

11th Grade

Subject	Grade	Test	Score	GPA/Class Rank	Awards and Honors
English		PSAT			
		7. Critical Reading			
		8. Math			
		9. Writing			
Math		SAT (current)			
		5. Math			
		6. Verbal			
		New SAT (class of 2006) 7. Critical Reading			
Science		8. Math			
		9. Writing			
		AP			
Social		7.			
Studies		8.			
		9.			

12th Grade

Subject	Grade	Test	Score	GPA/Class Rank	Awards and Honors
English		PSAT			
		10. Critical Reading			
		11. Math			
		12. Writing			
Math		SAT (current)			
		7. Math			
		8. Verbal			
		New SAT (class of 2006) 10. Critical Reading			
Science		11. Math			
		12. Writing			
		AP			
Social		10.			
Studies		11.			
		12.			

STUDENT RESUME

It is worthwhile to work on a student resume for a number of reasons. Firstly, you can give your resume to your school counselor who will probably be writing your school recommendation. Secondly, you should offer your resume to any teacher or any other person who will be writing a recommendation for you. Thirdly, the resume will help you when you work on your college applications.

You will notice that a great deal of emphasis in this resume is put on accomplishments. One of the biggest errors on job resumes is that job seekers don't list their accomplishments. Rather, they only showed where they worked and their responsibilities. But, how well did they fulfill those responsibilities? So, "talk" about whatever accomplishments you have achieved. This is not the time to win an award for modesty. However, you need to be honest all the way.

To help you out, here is a list of power words that will trigger your thoughts and remind you of things you have done at school and in the community. Use this list and even brainstorm with the family.

POWER WORDS

Need some strong words to get you thinking about accomplishments and responsibilities? Here is a list of words below that may trigger your memory. For example, looking at the word "sold", one student realized that she sold more ads for the school publication than anyone else in the student body, and the word "organized" reminded another student that she organized an event to raise money for charity. Just think; ideas will start coming your way. For each activity you listed in this document, look over the list of words for those that may help you see what you accomplished in that activity.

achieved	administered	advised	analyzed	arranged
budgeted	campaigned	communicated	completed	conducted
coordinated	counseled	created	contributed	critiqued
computed	determined	developed	designed	devised
directed	established	excited	evaluated	executed
explored	formulated	gathered	generated	guided
illustrated	implemented	improved	initiated	instituted
instructed	introduced	invented	launched	managed
motivated	operated	organized	participated	performed
planned	prepared	presented	presided	programmed
produced	promoted	recommended	researched	reviewed
revised	reorganized	selected	sold	solved
scheduled	supervised	taught	trained	tutored

STUDENT RESUME

NAME:
ADDRESS:
CITY, STATE, ZIP:
TELEPHONE NUMBER:
E-MAIL ADDRESS:
SOCIAL SECURITY NUMBER:
HIGH SCHOOL NAME:
HIGH SCHOOL ADDRESS:
HIGH SCHOOL COUNSELOR:
EXPECTED GRADUATION DATE:

ACADEMICS

GRADE POINT AVERAGE: CLASS RANK:
HIGHEST SAT I:
     VERBAL: MATH: DATE TAKEN:
HIGHEST SAT II:
     SUBJECT: SCORE: DATE TAKEN:
     SUBJECT: SCORE: DATE TAKEN:
     SUBJECT: SCORE: DATE TAKEN:

AP and/or HONORS, COLLEGE COURSES, COLLEGE SUMMER PROGRAM:

_____
_____
_____
_____

EXTRACURRICULAR ACTIVITIES:

ACTIVITY/POSITIONS   **GRADE(S)**   **LEADERSHIP**
ACCOMPLISHMENTS _____
_____

ACTIVITY/POSITIONS   **GRADE(S)**   **LEADERSHIP**
ACCOMPLISHMENTS _____
_____

COMMUNITY ACTIVITIES:

ACTIVITY/POSITIONS   **GRADE(S)**   **LEADERSHIP**
ACCOMPLISHMENTS _____
_____

ACTIVITY/POSITIONS   **GRADE(S)**   **LEADERSHIP**
ACCOMPLISHMENTS _____
_____

AWARDS AND HONORS:

AWARD NAME	DATE RECEIVED	SIGNIFICANCE/EXPLANATION
1.		
2.		
3.		

WORK EXPERIENCE:

JOB TITLE	BUSINESS NAME	EMPLOYMENT DATES
1.		
2.		
3.		

INTERESTS AND HOBBIES: _____

_____

MAJOR TRAVEL EXPERIENCES: _____

_____

OTHER COMMENTS: _____

_____

_____

SIZING UP SCHOOLS

Now that you know more about yourself, it is time to find out just what you want from a college. Complete the checklist titled, "What I Want From a College," and check off every answer that applies. Do not be surprised if you have more than one space checked under a given category. This is your checklist, no one else's. Again, take your time. You will be using the checklist as a measuring stick to "size up" each college you consider.

I. What I Want from a College (Check/Answer All Categories That Apply):

Location	
Urban	
Suburban	
Rural	
Geographic Area	
New England	
Mid-Atlantic	
South	
Midwest	
West coast	
Abroad	
Affiliation	
State	
Private	
Military	
Religious	
Other	

Enrollment	
Very Small (under 1,000)	
Small (1,000 to 5,000)	
Medium (5,000 to 10,000)	
Large (over 10,000)	
Student Body	
Co-ed	
All women	
All men	
Academic Program	
Liberal Arts	
Teacher Training	
Technical	
Pre-Professional	
Term of Study	
4- Year College	
2- Year College	
Other	

Enrollment	
Scholarship	
Loans	
Employment	

Extra-Curricular Outlet

Athletic Programs

Social Life Opportunities

II. What I Want from a College: Other Needs (Check/Answer All Categories That Apply)

3-2 Engineering Program (three years of liberal arts at one school, two years engineering at another)	
Accelerated Program (complete college in less than four years)	
Acceptance to Graduate or Professional School at Time of Admission (e.g., Medical School, Law School, MBA, Dental School)	
Conservative Student Body	
Ethnic and Religious Diversity	
Exchange Programs with Other Colleges	
Historically Black College	
Independent Research with Professor	
Learning Disability	
Liberal Student Body	
No Core or Distribution Requirements	
Student Government	
Study Abroad	

RESOURCES

If you are sure of the kind of college you are looking for, then go on to the next step—scanning every college guide, handbook and catalog that you can find. Here is a list of works that will help you:

Barron's Profiles of American Colleges, 2004. Barron's Educational Series: 250 Wireless Blvd., Hauppauge NY 11788; (800) 645-3476. 1648 pp; $26.95. Two volumes, updated every two years, offers information on over 1,650 colleges in the United States.

Campus Visits and College Interviews, 2002. Zola Dincin Schneider, College Board: 45 Columbus Ave., New York, NY 10023-6992; (212) 713-8000. 125 pp; $12.95. This guide prepares students for college visits and interviews by giving helpful tips on what to look for and what interviewers look for.

College Handbook 2005, annual. College Board; 2036 pp; $27.95. This 42nd edition is a comprehensive reference offering descriptions of 3,600 colleges, with objective and current data on each college, with additional tables and graphs for supplement.

Fiske College Deadline Planner 2004-2005, annual. Edward B. Fisk, Bruce G. Hammond, Sourcebooks, Inc.: 1935 Brookdale Rd., Suite 139, Naperville, IL 60563; (800) 43-BRIGHT. 192 pp; $14.95. Covering a 16-month period, this useful planner helps relieve the stress in the admission process by detailing important deadlines.

The Fiske Guide to Colleges, annual. Edward B. Fiske, Sourcebooks, Inc.; 765 pp; $22.95. This guidebook offers information on more than 330 colleges, giving a mix of statistical data and personal accounts.

The Fiske Guide to Getting into the Right College, 2002. Edward B. Fiske, Bruce G. Hammond, Sourcebooks, Inc.; 257 pp; $14.95. Helps students get into the college of their choice, offering advice on the how-to's of the admission process

The Insider's Guide to Colleges, 2005, annual. Yale Daily News, St. Martin's Griffin: 175 Fifth Ave., New York, NY 10010. 992 pp; $17.99. This guide, covering over 300 top colleges, is written by students.

K & W Guide to Colleges for Students with Learning Disabilities or Attention Deficit Disorder, 2003. Imy F. Wax, Marybeth Kravets, Princeton Review: 2315 Broadway, New York, NY 10024; (212) 874-8282). 816 pp; $27.00. Provides information on 338 schools, in addition to advice and services available to students with learning disabilities.

National Association of College Admission Counselors: 1631 Prince St., Alexandria, VA 22314-2818; (703) 836-2222.
Guide for Parents. Free
Guide to the College Admission Process. $5.00
Web Resources for the College-Bound. $5.00

Octameron Associates: P.O. Box 2748, Alexandria, VA 22301; (703) 836-5480.
Behind the Scenes: An Inside Look at the Selective College Admission Process. $7.00
Campus Pursuit: Making the Most of Your Visit and Interview. $5.00
College Match: A Blueprint for Choosing the Best School for You! $10.00
Do It—Write: How to Prepare a Great College Application. $6.00
College-Planning Guide: A Free Brochure for Students and Parents.

Peterson's Guides, Peterson's: 2000 Lenox Drive, P.O. Box 67005, Lawrenceville, NJ 08648; (800) 338-3282.
Colleges for Students with Learning Disabilities or Add, 2003. 650 pp; $29.95. Offers in-depth information on more than 750 schools in the United States and Canada for students with special needs.
Peterson's Four-Year Colleges, annual. 3091 pp; $29.95. Contains information on more than 2,100 colleges across the United States and Canada, with detailed descriptions of almost 1,000 colleges. Includes bonus CD ROM with additional information.
Peterson's Two-Year Colleges, annual. 738 pp; $24.95. Includes information on nearly 1,800 institutions across the country, and details on every facet of the college selection and admission process.
Peterson's Honor Programs, 2002. Joan Digby; 634 pp; $24.95. Complete overview of honors programs and scholarships in more than 450 schools, including advice from the President of the National Collegiate Honors Council.

Unofficial, Unbiased Guide to the 331 Most Interesting Colleges 2005, annual. Kaplan: 888 7th Ave., New York, NY 10106; (212) 492-5800. 720 pp; $19.00. Full of helpful information like guidance counselors' reports and personal college accounts, as well as standard admission information.

U.S. News Ultimate College Directory, annual. Anne McGrath, Robert J. Morse, Sourcebooks, Inc. 1400 pp; $29.95. A comprehensive directory from the education information experts, this guide covers more than 1,400 colleges and focuses on such essential reports as school rankings, costs, and deadlines.

What It Really Takes to Get Into Ivy League and Other Highly Selective Colleges, 2003. Chuck Hughes, McGraw-Hill: P.O. Box 182604, Columbus OH 43272; (877) 833-5524. 288 pp; $16.95. Written by a former Harvard University admission officer, this guide offers a breakdown of the components of a successful application, including extra-curriculars and personality traits.

SUMMER PROGRAMS

Signing up for a summer program may not sound very appealing at first. But summer programs offer enormous benefits. Think of it this way. Summer programs give you the opportunity to check out campuses, meet people with similar interests, do something more exciting than watching reruns of South Park and hanging out at Dairy Queen, keep your parents from nagging at you so much, and increase your chances of getting into the college of your choice.

The bad thing about summer programs is that they're offered at so many colleges that it's impossible to list them all. The good thing is that you can bet that almost any school you're interested in will have something going for high school students over the summer. Two books that list various summer programs across the nation and can help you enormously are 1) *Guide to Summer Camps & Summer Schools*, published by Porter Sargent Publishers, Inc., 2) *Kaplan Yale Daily News Guide to Summer Programs*, published by Kaplan, and 3) *Summer Opportunities for Kids and Teenagers, 2004* published by Peterson's. Peterson's website (http:// www.petersons.com/) includes a searchable database of summer programs. Don't be misled by the titles of the books, because "camps" include both academic and study abroad programs.

There are three main types of summer programs: 1) academic programs, 2) college admission/ experience programs, and 3) exchange/study abroad programs. It's a good idea to clarify in your own mind which type of program best fits your needs or interests. Are you hoping to overcome an academic weakness? Do you want to experience campus life and learn how to apply to college? Are you interested in doing advanced work in a particular topic? Do you want to earn college credit? Or are you trying to figure out if a particular career suits you? Knowing what you want to achieve will enable you to choose the summer program that's best for you, and ensure that you'll have a worthwhile experience once you do. Your high school counselor should be a good source of information. Surfing the web will give you tons of information too.

Tip: Keep in mind that college summer programs for high school students are not conducted every year at every college (often because of funding or enrollment problems). Therefore, it's advisable to check them out as soon as possible. Competition can be rather intense for some programs.

ACADEMIC PROGRAMS

There are three types of academic programs:
  A) Programs for students who want to do higher level work (and perhaps earn college credit)
  B) Programs designed for students who need extra help in an academic subject
  C) Programs to help students explore potential careers

A. HIGHER WORK

If you already have a passion for a particular field and want to do higher level work in it, or if you're hoping to meet other students with similar interests, you may want to enroll in a summer program that emphasizes advanced work. Often these programs are for gifted students, but don't worry if you're not an Einstein–sometimes the programs aren't graded, so they can be a great way to learn without the pressure of competition for good grades. (Of course, if you're in a program that awards college credit you can expect to be graded.) Examples:

American Computer Experience (ACE) runs computer camps at various colleges across the country. For the location closest to you, contact ACE at ace@computercamp.com

Birmingham-Southern College, Birmingham, AL offers a Summer Scholars Program. Scholars get free tuition for two college level courses and are responsible only for their housing and book costs. http://www.bsc.edu/

Harvard University, Cambridge, MA enrolls about 1,000 high school students each summer who take classes alongside undergraduates and earn college credit. http://ssp.dce.harvard.edu/

B. ACADEMIC ENRICHMENT/REMEDIAL WORK

These programs either emphasize skills (like studying techniques) that will enrich your academic experience or they help you work on a particular weakness. Often the program includes a component on SAT or ACT preparation. Examples:

Choate-Rosemary Hall School, Wallingford, CT is a private high school that offers a wide range of high school subjects, as well as an intensive writing course for the student who wants to improve writing skills. http://www.choate.edu/summer/HS/hsindex.html

Northwestern University, Evanston, IL holds a College Writing Tutorial during its summer program to help students develop their writing skills prior to entering college. Go to http://www.northwestern.edu/, then click on Site Index, then click on H, then click on High School Institute, National

SuperCamp helps students "learn to learn" while attending an eight to ten day camp at prestigious college campuses throughout the US. If your school habits need improving, contact http://www.supercamp.com/

Tip: There's nothing shameful in doing remedial work. Being smart enough to see that you have a weakness in an academic area like writing or math, and doing something about it will pay off greatly during your college years.

C. EXPLORATION OF CAREER FIELDS

Do you think you'd like to be a marine biologist, but you've never even seen the ocean? Or perhaps you want to be a journalist, but have no idea what the inside of a newspaper office looks like? Then a program that explores potential career fields is for you. Contact colleges and universities that have good reputations in your career choice. Examples:

Academy of Art College, San Francisco, CA. If you're artistic and would like to explore the various opportunities in visual arts prior to making a career or educational choice, check out the Academy at http://www.academyart.edu/specgen.html

University of Miami, Miami, FL. Summer Scholars Program. Explore a potential career field like marine sciences by visiting local work sites, taking classes, and earning college credit. Email ssp.cstudies@miami.edu for more information.

Stanford University, Stanford, CA runs a program to introduce gifted low-income, primarily minority, high school students to environmental issues and related careers. http://questscholars.stanford.edu/

COLLEGE ADMISSION/COLLEGE EXPERIENCE

This type of summer program lets high school students experience what campus life is like, explore various colleges and universities, prepare a college admission packet, and prep for the SAT or ACT. Academic work (either higher level or remedial) is not emphasized, nor is career exploration, but occasionally there is still an opportunity to take a college credit course or two.

Examples:

University of Wisconsin, Madison, WI offers American Collegiate Adventures. Students visit campuses in Michigan, Minnesota, Indiana and Illinois. SAT/ACT prep and two college level courses are included. http://www.acasumr.com/

Collegiate Guidance Council's college admission camps are held at top colleges every year on a rotating basis. You spend nine days working on college interview skills, admission essays, and choosing the right college for you. 1-800-548-6612

EXCHANGE/STUDY ABROAD

Exchange or study abroad programs give you a unique opportunity to experience a different culture, either by living with a host family or on a college campus in a foreign country. The focus of these programs can be academic learning, language immersion, or community or environmental service. Some programs will expect you to have already studied a foreign language.

Usually a variety of full-year, semester, and summer programs is available. You will also find that full and partial scholarships, along with loans, are offered by various organizations.

A good source when trying to find an exchange or travel abroad program is Peterson's *Summer Fun: Travel and International Camps*. Peterson's website (http://www.petersons.com/) includes a searchable database of programs.

Tip: Unless your study abroad program takes place in Mexico or Canada, you'll probably need a passport. The US State Department has a terrific website to answer your passport questions, and even includes a printable passport application. See http://www.travel.state.gov/ for more information.

Examples of some exchange and study abroad programs are:

Cambridge College Programme, Cambridge, England has a pre-college academic and cultural enrichment summer program. If you'd like to live on campus in jolly old England and attend lectures by British professors, call 1-800-922-3552.

Earthwatch, Maynard, MA runs over 100 environmental expeditions every year at locations around the world. You'll work in the field assisting scientists with research and conservation activities. Scholarships are available for high school students. http://www.earthwatch.org/

Experiment in International Living, Brattleboro, VT promotes cross-cultural understanding by placing high school students in host families throughout the world. http://www.experiment.org/

COLLEGE SHOPPING LIST

Now that you know yourself better, you are ready to investigate potential colleges. You probably find yourself more equipped to make better choices since you took a good look at who you are and what you want. Now your task is to find 10 to 15 schools that measure up to the profile that you developed in the previous section of this book.

With information from your college handbooks and guides, you can fill out your College Shopping List on the next few pages. Write down each school's name, full address, and enrollment size. Then, write the mid-50 percent SAT range or ACTs. You can also use averages. Include average GPAs for each school. Finally, include one fact or reason for consideration or important thing about the school. This is your tentative list of "possibles."

Then, to help you further in your analysis of each school, we have included several "Pros and Cons Worksheets" as well.

Name & Address of School	Size	Tuition	Room & Board	Books & Fees	Cost Per Year
	One Interesting or Important Thing About the School:				
Name & Address of School	Size	Tuition	Room & Board	Books & Fees	Cost Per Year
	One Interesting or Important Thing About the School:				
Name & Address of School	Size	Tuition	Room & Board	Books & Fees	Cost Per Year
	One Interesting or Important Thing About the School:				
Name & Address of School	Size	Tuition	Room & Board	Books & Fees	Cost Per Year
	One Interesting or Important Thing About the School:				

Name of School	Average SAT	Average GPA	Other Requirements	Other interesting and important facts about enrollment

PROS AND CONS WORKSHEET

Use this format for comparing and contrasting the schools on your College Shopping List.

Name	Address of School

ACADEMICS	PROS	CONS
Curriculum and Coursework		
Faculty		
Special Programs (e.g. exchange programs, dual-degrees, foreign programs, internships)		

	PROS	CONS
Size		
Location		
Organizations and Athletics		
Financial Aid Availability		
Social Life		
Post-Graduate Opportunities		
Alumni Activities		
Other Considerations (i.e. Housing, Career Placement)		

QUICK SELECTION QUIZ

Important Questions to Evaluate Colleges Further:

	Yes	No	Excellent	Good	Fair
1. Has the college received accreditation from the regional Association of Colleges and Secondary Schools?					
2. Are my philosophy and goals on education compatible with the college?					
3. Is the college state-supported, private or sectarian (sponsored by a religious denomination)?					
4. Are religious courses required?					
5 Is chapel attendance required?					
6. Is cooperative education offered?					
7. What is the make-up of the college's population according to sex, race and geographic origins?					
8. Can the campus be easily reached by public transportation?					
9. What kind of expenses will be incurred traveling back and forth?					
10. In what part of the country is the college located?					
11. In what kind of neighborhood is the school situated?					
12. Can I choose an interdepartmental major?					
13. Can I design my own major?					
14. How flexible are the course requirements for my desired degree?					

SELECTIVITY RATINGS

Terms like selectivity rating or selectivity level refer to the admission policy of colleges based on their applicants' median standardized test scores, class rank and grade point averages. Some schools are termed highly selective or highly competitive while others are described as non-selective. Here's a sample of schools in each selectivity level:

Schools	Selectivity Rating
Brown University Duke University Harvey Mudd College University of Michigan University of Notre Dame Swarthmore College	Most competitive (Fewer than 30% accepted)
Agnes Scott College Carleton College Illinois Institute of Technology Rutgers, the State U. of N.J. The University of the South Whitman College	Very competitive (Fewer than 60% accepted)
American Academy of Dramatic Arts Arizona State University Bowling Green State University Fisk University Howard University Texas A & M University	Moderately competitive (85% accepted)
Alabama State University Florida A & M University The Newport College—Salve Regina	Less-competitive (95%) accepted)
Montana State University Ohio State University—Columbus Pan American University	Non-competitive (98%) accepted)

SAMPLE LETTERS

Remember that what you write makes an impression on the college, so be sure your letters are neat and legible. The college may start its file on you by placing your first letter in it.

Sample Information Request Letter:

Date

Your Name
Your Street Address
Your Town, State, Zip Code

Director of Admission
Name of School
P.O. Box or Other Office Address
City, State, Zip Code

Dear Mr. or Mrs. X:

I am a junior *[sophomore, senior]* at _____ High School and am interested in knowing more about _____College [or University].

I would appreciate your sending to me 1. Your most recent college catalog, 2. An application for admission, 3. Financial aid information, 4. A video or CD of your institution, if available, and 5. any other pertinent materials.

I would also like information about _____
(Examples: specific majors, athletics, particular organizations).

Thank you for taking care of my request.

Sincerely,

Your Signature

Printed Name

Sample Campus Visit Request Letter:

Date

Your Name
Your Street Address
Your Town, State, Zip Code

Director of Admission
Name of School
P.O. Box or Other Office Address
City, State, Zip Code

Dear Mr. or Mrs. X:

I am a junior at Lakewood High School in Anytown, RI and would like to visit your campus between July 15 and 16.

My particular interest is in your agricultural program. Is it possible to meet with a faculty member in that area as well as take a tour of the campus and talk with an admission department representative? Since I am applying for financial aid, I would appreciate having a chance to talk with someone from that office also.

Please let me know if these dates are convenient. If not, I can arrange to visit during any Tuesday or Wednesday in July.

Sincerely,

Your Signature

Printed Name

Sample Thank-You Letter:

Date

Your Name
Your Street Address
Your Town, State, Zip Code

Director of Admission
Name of School
P.O. Box or Other Office Address
City, State, Zip Code

Dear Mr. or Mrs. X:

I thoroughly enjoyed being on your campus last month, and am writing to thank you for arranging such a productive visit for me.

The opportunity to speak with Professor Livingston in your agriculture department was a highlight. I also was impressed with the friendliness of the students, and the opportunity to stay in the dormitory overnight was rather exciting.

I shall definitely be applying to Montana.

Sincerely,

Your Signature

Printed Name

TEST DATES

Make sure you have taken, by the end of your junior year, all of the exams necessary for college admission. These are the SAT I, ACT and SAT II subject tests.

Here are the usual months during which the tests are given. Those taking the tests on Sunday for religious reasons, note that the Sunday usually follows the Saturday testing. Once in a while there is an exception. By looking at the College Board and ACT websites fill in the test dates for this year.

DATE	SAT I	ACT	SAT II

STANDARDIZED TEST TIPS

The most important tip that can be given about a standardized test is to forget what you believe this tool is unless it agrees with the following.

Standardized tests measure verbal and mathematical reasoning abilities and have very little to do with natural intelligence. The abilities that are measured by standardized exams have been developed usually over a period of years and *may* have some relationship to academic performance in college.

The big question is often, "How should I prepare for a standardized test?" Of course the answer is simple.

- Develop verbal and writing skills in English.

- Improve your understanding of mathematics.

- Work with vocabulary lists and grammar texts on your own or with friends.

- Take advantage of standardized test preparation guides which will acquaint you with the format and procedure of the text.

- Special preparation programs are an option that must involve consideration of cost and time diverted from other activities in your life.

None of these tips will do any good if you wait until the last week to initiate them. They must be several months in the working.

Get sufficient sleep on the night before the test. Don't try to cram—it won't do you any good at this point. And in the morning, give yourself plenty of time to dress and eat so that you can arrive at the test site a bit early. Go for it!

RECOMMENDATION LETTERS

Most colleges also require recommendation letters from current teachers, a guidance counselor and an administrator. After four years of high school, you know which teachers and administrators you can trust to write the best letters on your behalf.

But to be on the safe side, ask the recommender what kind of letter will be sent. If the teacher cannot be very supportive, find another. Remember, it is *your* future, not theirs that is on the line. Nine out of ten times, your best teachers will write your best letters. But you can never be too careful. You want only the best impression to be received from your application—and you have every right to be concerned about what goes in it.

To get a more accurate meter of the teachers who offer to write recommendation letters, check with some of their former students. And in order to assist the teachers in drafting your letter smoothly, give them plenty of advance notice about deadlines.

Make sure to give your recommenders the form you received in the college application materials. If you are using the Internet, print out the recommendation form. Don't forget to include an envelope with a stamp on it, addressed to the college.

Remember the resume you completed earlier? Either use that completed resume or design your own, and give it to your recommenders. This will help your recommenders know more about you. They will probably appreciate the help.

Should you send additional recommendations beyond what is asked by the college? Only if you have a valid reason. Let's look at some examples. You want to major in communications and you worked at a TV studio over the summer. That could be appropriate. You want to go into teaching and you were a counselor at a camp. Sounds good. You want to go into the culinary arts and you cut grass over the summer. Not appropriate. Perhaps, you were particularly outstanding in an extra-curricular activity, or you want an athletic coach to write, or an employer where you made a solid contribution. That could be fine. The mayor, governor or senator. Not fine. The college knows that they don't know you. They only know your family's political contribution. If you worked in the office of a government official, that's a different story.

ESSAY DO'S AND DON'TS

Some schools ask that you write about a current event or issue. Other colleges want you to write about your personal goals and ambitions. Still others ask you to write about your favorite book.

These required essays have two purposes. First the college wants to assess your ability to write clearly. Secondly, the college wants to learn something about your ability to think clearly.

There is no one way to write a good personal essay, but following is a list of some do's and don'ts that will help you prepare your best composition.

DOs	DON'Ts
→ Write down main idea before composing	→ Use slang
→ Write clearly-if it sounds vague, change it.	→ Try to be "cute."
→ Use words you are comfortable with.	→ Use words that you can't define.
→ Express, not impress.	→ Begin your essay with "My name is..."
→ Edit and rewrite until your essay says what you mean.	→ Digress from the original topic.
→ Let your English teacher proofread your essay.	→ Go on for more than the specified length.
→ Check all spelling and grammar.	→ Be too general. Focus on one meaningful episode rather than a complete history.
→ Give yourself plenty of time.	→ Beg
→ Understand what an essay is (check a dictionary).	→ Be afraid to give an opinion or make a point.
→ Answer all questions.	

SEND SAMPLES

In addition to the essay, you may want to send the college demonstrations—art portfolios, writing samples—of outstanding talent. Be sure your supplementary materials are of exceptional quality, and be certain to check with the college about how and when to send the materials.

Do not try to "snow" the college admission committee. If you are not a current member of the chess club or math club or computer club, do not put it down as an activity. If all you enjoy is collecting different species of weeds and classifying them, then put it down! Remember, depth of involvement is more important than quantity. Make your application reflect *you*. Use your creative juices—be innovative, but honest.

THE INTERVIEW

Many colleges recommend interviews. A large percentage of these are private, highly selective schools. However, if you want to make a good impression, don't wait for the admission office to invite you to campus.

Contact the college and offer to make an appointment. This request will be acceptable because many colleges don't have a standing policy about interviews. They wait for ambitious candidates to schedule one on their own. In some cases, colleges have alumni doing the interviews in your area. The interview is one area where you can make an impression and a "face" can be attached to your application. It is important to be prepared for the interview. This means being ready to respond to the interviewer's questions and being ready to ask good questions. Note that some schools don't have individual interviews but group sessions. You still have an opportunity to ask questions.

Be prepared to answer and ask some personally relevant questions. Try not to ask questions that are already answered in the materials you received from the college. A poor question is do you have fraternities and sororities? The answer to that question can be found in the college's literature. Asking that question only proves that either you can't read, don't comprehend what you read, or didn't bother to read the literature that the college spent money on so that you, a prospective student, would know the answer.

Here are some questions you should consider:

1. Specifically, what is the professional reputation of individual faculty members in the department (in which you are interested)?
2. Do students tend to live off-campus in the upper-class years?
3. What grading system is being used? Do students work primarily for grades?
4. What are class attendance requirements?
5. What school-sponsored activities exist solely for freshmen?
6. What kinds of social events are sponsored by the college during the year?
7. What is the typical recreation for students during the week or on weekends?
8. Is there any information on the percentage of students who leave campus for the entire weekend?
9. Do the fraternities and sororities control social life on campus? (This assumes that there is a Greek system)
10. Does the college offer cultural enrichment programs on a regular basis?
11. For which sports do the students support their teams?
12. What health services are available?
13. Can the library meet most of my needs?
14. What changes are on the drawing boards either in the curriculum or physical facilities?
15. What is the average class size for freshman?
16. How much interaction do faculty and students have outside the classroom?
17. What areas of the college need improvement to make it an even better college?
18. What opportunities are there for research by students?
19. Have there been any hot issues on campus in the past few years?
20. Does one's choice of major affect the admission process?
21. What is the reputation of the career guidance center?
22. What are the pros and cons of different housing options?
23. How does the advising system work?

24. How secure are the dormitories? Are they single sex...coed...? How many students are housed in each room?

25. Where are the computers located, and during which hours are they accessible?

QUESTIONS INTERVIEWERS ASK

During the college interview process, you'll come across interviewers who will ask you hundreds of questions. Many are basic questions, but are used to steer the conversation in a particular direction. In other words, most of the typical "yes" or "no" questions will require more than a simple "yes" or "no." You should expect to explain what you say. Here are some frequently recurring questions for which you should be prepared.

1. Why do you wish to attend our college?
2. What will you offer the college after you enroll?
3. What do you think you'll be doing 10 years from now?
4. What was you most valuable experience during your high school years?
5. If you were granted three wishes, for what would you ask?
6. How do you spend your free time?
7. What are the most important things that high school has taught you?
8. What is your opinion about [an issue of current interest]?
9. What do you like and dislike about your high school?
10. What magazines and newspapers do you read? How often? What is the focus of your reading?
11. Describe your innermost fears.
12. What events have been crucial in your life?
13. What are your weaknesses or in what areas would you like to improve?
14. What classes have you enjoyed most? Why?
15. What has been your most worthwhile summer?
16. What books or articles have had an impact on your thinking?
17. What would your teachers say were your greatest strengths and your shortcomings or weaknesses?
18. Where and when do you find yourself most stimulated intellectually?
19. What will be the "good life" for you twenty years from now?
20. By what five adjectives would your friends describe you?

THE CAMPUS VISIT

It's time to get to know the college firsthand. Reading about a college is necessary. Talking about a college is a definite plus. But visiting a college—seeing, smelling and tasting a college—is invaluable. If it is impossible for you to visit a college (travel expenses can get steep), call the admission office and arrange for an interview with an alumnus (male) or alumna (female) of the college who may be located in your area. What do you do once you find yourself in the middle of a strange college campus? Here are some pertinent pointers:

• The visit should be scheduled several weeks in advance. For more popular schools, give yourself a few months.

- Before you visit, make an appointment to meet with an admission counselor.

- Give enough advance notice so that you will be able to stay overnight with students in a dormitory room, if your schedule permits. Otherwise, visit again if you are accepted and spend more time at the college, if it is one of your final choices.

- Plan to visit during the academic year, when campus life is in full swing. However, you may have more time during the summer months but the disadvantage is that the usual students aren't on campus. The advantage is that you have the time.

- Go with your parents. They often ask the questions that you feel uncomfortable asking (e.g., "What kind of security is available on campus?" or "Are drugs a problem on campus?"), but you'll want to have some time on your own. If you plan to stay overnight, make arrangements for your parents to stay at a motel or hotel.

- Arrange for a campus tour and stay close to the tour guide; listen to the side comments as well as the "spiel."

- Visit as many classes as possible, especially those in your area of interest.

- Ask professors questions relating to the course, the assignments, and their field of interest.

- Talk to several students in the classes you attend about their academic interests.

- Take notes as you go about the environment, facilities, faculty, size of classes, living conditions, student body and any "vibes" you get.

- Eat in the dining hall, not only to get a taste of the food, but also to get a candid view of the students.

FINISHING TOUCHES

There are a number of ways to file applications to colleges. The most traditional is the written application. At one time, that was the only method of applying. In our computer and Internet age, there are alternative ways to apply. Some colleges have their own online applications.

Then there is the common application where about 250 colleges agree to use the same application. You only have to copy the original each time you apply to one of the colleges in the program. But be careful, colleges may have a supplemental form or two which must be completed. It is an easier way to apply and colleges claim that they don't discriminate against students who use the common app rather than their own college application. In fact, they have signed an agreement that they will treat the commonapp on an equal status as their own application.

From year to year, there are services on the Internet that you can do online to replicate a given college's application. Remember, there are various parts to most applications some of which you need to give to your school and teachers.

- Make sure you ask and answer the all-important question, "Could I be happy and successful at a given college?"

- Send a thank-you note to the director of admission and the admission officer who interviewed you. See the thank-you letter on an earlier page. This expression of courtesy will probably be placed in your file.

- Locate the student job office to see what kinds of employment are available.

- Visit the library. Are students studying or just checking out books? How large is the periodical section? Are there quiet areas to study?

- Find some back copies of the campus newspaper to see what issues are key and what students are saying.

- How close is the town? Will you need transportation? Are movies, restaurants and entertainment nearby?

MY APPLICATION FOLLOW-UP

This checklist will help you organize the application process. Some of the items may not be applicable to a given college.

YOUR NAME: _____

NAME OF SCHOOL: _____

ADMISSION ADDRESS: _____

IMPORTANT DEADLINES	DUE DATE	COMPLETED
Application: Part One		
Application: Part Two (if applicable)		
College Financial Aid Deadline		
FAFSA (Free Application for Federal Student Aid)		
College's Merit Scholarship Competition		

APPLICATION	TARGET/DUE DATE	COMPLETED
Requested		
Received		
Target Date to Complete		
Personal Information		
Short Answer		
Essay		
Total Application Proofread		
Sent to College (including application fee)		

REQUEST HIGH SCHOOL TO SEND	DATE	COMPLETED
Transcript		
School Recommendation		
Mid-Year Report		
Final Transcript		

TEACHER RECOMMENDATIONS	DATE	CONFIRMED SENT
Given To:		
Given To:		
Given To:		

TEST SCORES	DATE REQUESTED	
Requested College Board to send SAT Scores to College		
Requested College Board to send ACT Scores to College		
SAT II scores Released *(if Score Choice used)*		

FINANCIAL AID	YES	YES	DATE REQUESTED
FAFSA Filed			
FAFSA Report Received			
College's Own Financial Aid Form Filed			

INTERVIEW	YES	No	DATE & TIME SCHEDULED
Required			
Recommended			

VISIT TO COLLEGE	YES	No	DATE & TIME SCHEDULED
Appointment Made			
Visits Complete			

COLLEGE DECISION		DATE NOTIFIED
Accepted		
Denied		
Wait List		
Deferred from Early Decision		

FOLLOW UP	DATE
Notify College of Decision to Attend	
Notify College of Decision not to Attend	

ACCEPTED? DENIED? WAITLISTED?

Any one of three decisions will be rendered when the admission office makes a decision on your application. You may be accepted which will be to your delight, denied which you didn't want to hear, or waitlisted hoping to secure a spot in the class if room opens up after May 1.

If you applied early decision (a binding option), you can be accepted, denied or put into the regular pool for the spring. The same holds true for early action (a non-binding option).

If you are accepted to a given college at any point, you have until May 1 to tell them of your decision to attend. However, Early Decision candidates are bound to attend a college that accepts them and you need to adhere to the rules of that college.

The rejection letter comes to the homes of thousands of high school students from the admission officers of the college of their first, second and sometimes even third choice.

"Why?" is the question that occurs most frequently. Despite reduced enrollments at private colleges, an estimated 100 of the nation's 1400 four-year private undergraduate institutions receive twice as many applications as they can accept. And in some cases, the ratio is higher. In the very competitive colleges, only 1 or 2 of every ten applicants is accepted. Nothing is wrong with the 8 or 9 students who get denial letters. However, the college only has room for a certain number of students.

Several admission officers will admit that they often reject highly qualified students. Further, they deal with favoritism toward children of alumni, outstanding athletes and toward applicants in certain racial, geographic, ethnic and other groups as they attempt to balance the student population.

A good rule of thumb for applicants to competitive schools is to have realistic expectations and apply to a variety of colleges with different admission standards. Sometimes, the school with the easier (not easy) standard may be the best college for you for a host of reasons. Have you really searched out your reasons for applying to a particular college? Are you attracted because your father or mother or even relative went there? Or do you really think that your career will have a better chance of taking off from that institution?

The effects of being denied by your first choice in colleges will not be disastrous unless you allow the rejection to eat away at you. Not always getting what you want is a fact of life. If you don't get your first choice, brush it off and go to another choice. With the proper attitude you can still take advantage of the best life has to offer. There are many fine colleges where you can succeed.

COLLEGE PLANNING CALENDAR

The application process can seem like a never-ending contest of you against the colleges. It can get complicated and frustrating. What do you do? Whom do you see?

To simplify the process, we have provided a College Planning Calendar to take you step-by-step, from selection to application to acceptance. Hang it on a wall in your room or put it in your own college-planning folder. This calendar is designed to keep you on track as you make your way from junior year to senior year—college bound all the way! For the SATs and ACTs you need to check the current test dates and deadlines in advance. You may want to include the deadlines for the tests you are going to take by adding them to the calendar. Get advice from your counselor and teachers about which tests you want to take and in what month.

COLLEGE PLANNING CALENDAR (Jr. & Sr. Years)

January	February	March	April
SATs	ACT	SAT I only	ACT
Begin "Factors" Inventory	Complete "Factors" Inventory	Develop list of potential colleges with your counselor and any other advisors	Plan campus visits
	Complete "Self Inventory"		Write for applications
	Complete "Values and Needs"	Send for college catalogs	Check senior year courses
	Meet with your counselor	Scan college guides	
		Attend college fairs and meetings	

May/June	July/August	September	October
SAT	Visit colleges and interviews	ACT in some states	SAT/ ACT
Visit colleges and interviews	Have a constructive summer	Start working on applications	Recommendation letters to teachers
Write for additional applications	Narrow your college list	especially for state schools	Complete any early decision or early action applications
AP exams			Arrange for any needed interviews including alumni interviews
SAT		Note scholarship deadlines	
ACT			
Visit colleges and interviews		Meet with your counselor	

November	December	January	February
Work on private college applications and complete any remaining state school applications	SAT	SAT (if needed)	Analyze your college choices
	ACT	Early Decision II applications due	
	Watch those deadlines	Start and try to finish FAFSA	Continue visiting colleges
Make copies of all applications	Plan possible college visits during vacation		Have Mid-term or semester grades sent to colleges
Note all deadlines	Complete all applications		Finish FAFSA
			Complete Profile

March	April	May	June
Keep your grades up. Avoid "senioritis"	Review each college that says "yes" and review financial aid packages.	You must accept a college by May 1.	Congratulations graduate!
Spring decisions will be coming in March and April	Notify your final choice where you will attend by May 1	Keep the grades up for waitlisted students, see if there is anything else you need to do to strengthen your application	Start preparing for college

Overview

One of the major hurdles in the college application process is financial aid. Few parents can afford to spend $20,000-$30,000 or more per year for their son's or daughter's college education. Economic reports always show college costs on the rise. This information leads many parents to the conclusion that they cannot afford to send their children to the top schools. But that may not be the case, considering the number of scholarships, grants, student loans and work-study programs available for students with financial need. Do not assume you cannot afford to attend college—even the most costly schools!

Need

Need is the difference between your cost of education (tuition, fees, room, board, etc.) and the amount you and your family can afford to pay. Need is calculated by taking into consideration your family's income, assets and expenses. All of this information is entered on a financial aid application.

Forms

The most important form your family will complete is the Free Application for Federal Financial Aid, called the FAFSA. This form is required by all colleges. You may not submit this form until after January 1 of your senior year. It is available from your school's guidance office, usually in December of your senior year. It is also online which is the preferred way to go. The online version saves you a few weeks because the information is already ready for processing when you submit it online. There are some colleges that also require the College Profile, another financial aid form. Information about the profile can be found on the college board website. The names of colleges requiring the Profile can also be found on the site. Once in a while, a college may want additional information on their own form. Just make sure all required forms are completed.

Where's the Money?

The money is out there, in the form of scholarships, grants, loans and work-study. *The Financial Aid Overview* on the following pages lists the various types of student aid programs, the terms of eligibility, the amounts available and where to apply. This chart is not an exhaustive list, but it does outline the major resources of financial aid available for today's college-bound students. An excellent source for financial aid information is www.finaid.org.

FINANCIAL AID OVERVIEW

Scholarships	Eligibility	Approximate Amounts	Where to Apply
Pell Grant (Federal)	Undergraduates who are pursuing their first bachelor's degree, in financial need attending post-secondary school	Up to $2400/year	File Financial Aid Form (FAFSA) requesting submission to basic grant, or file separate Basic Grant application
Supplemental Education Opportunity Grants (SEOG, Federal)	Students of academic promise who are accepted for college study and who are in exceptional financial need. Undergraduates only.	Up to $4000/year	File FAF requesting submission to SEOG; file FAF between January 1 and March 1
War Orphans Educational Assistance (Federal)	Children of certain deceased or disabled veterans	Up to $220/month	Veterans Administration
Reserve Officers' Training Corp (ROTC)	Students enrolling in ROTC and who are academically qualified.	Tuition, fees, books, and monthly stipend	Air Force ROTC, Maxwell AFB, AL 36112. Army ROTC, Ft. Monroe, VA 23651. Navy ROTC, Office of Naval Personnel, Washington, DC 20370; Marine Corp Commandant Code MMRO-6 Hqs, UMSC, Washington, DC 20380
Veterans' Dependants Education Assistance	Any student between the ages of 18 and 26, if one parent has either died or was disabled as a result of service in the Armed Forces.	$3423/month for 45 months	Veteran Administration
Rehabilitation Programs	Students with disabilities	Tuition, fees, room & board, and training	State rehabilitation agencies
Other State Aid	Eligibility varies	Amount varies	State education department
Campus Scholarship Programs	Eligibility varies	Amount varies	College Financial Aid Office; college catalogue should list scholarships offered.
Guaranteed Student Loans (GLS, State)	Undergraduate or graduate students who qualify for aid using the needs test	Up to $4000/year for undergraduates, up to $7500/year for graduates	Banks, credit unions, savings and loan associations.

FINANCIAL AID OVERVIEW

Scholarships	Eligibility	Approximate Amounts	Where to Apply
Perkins Loans	Undergraduate or graduate students who meet financial need requirements established by the federal government.	Up to $4500 for first two years of undergraduate study; maximum of $9000 for 4 and 5 years of undergraduate study; $18,000 maximum for graduate study	File FAF between January 1 and March 1
Parents Loans for Undergraduate Student (PLUS, Federal)	Parents of full- or part-time undergraduate or graduate students, not based on need.	Up to $4000/year per child enrolled full-time, $20,000 maximum	Banks, credit unions, savings and loan associations
Supplemental Loans for Students (SLS)	Independent undergraduate or graduate/ professional students	Up to $4000/year, maximum of $20,000	FAF
Stafford Loans (Federal)	Undergraduate and graduate students enrolled at least half-time at colleges and proprietary or vocational institutions	$2625/year for 1st and 2nd year undergraduates; $4000 for 3rd year plus; $7500 for graduate students; 8% interest for first 4 years	FAF
Employment	All students	Amount varies	College financial aid office
College Work-Study Program	Undergraduates or graduates who meet financial need requirements established by the federal government	Amount varies, must be paid at least minimum wage	College financial aid office

FINANCIAL AID PACKAGES

Below are sample packages for students:

John Debe

John is from a family of four in New York State. His mother works in a bank and his father is a department store manager. Their approximate annual income is $45,000. They own a house with a small portion of the mortgage remaining. In addition, the family saving amounts to about $15,000. John is majoring in architecture, art and planning. His financial need list looks like this:

*Tuition, Room and Board, Books,
          Personal Expenses, and Travel $19,090

                    -Less John's Contribution $ 1,050
                    -Less Parents' Contribution $ 7,000

                    FINANCIAL NEED   **$11,040**

The college offered John and his family a financial aid package resembling this:

*College Work-Study $ 1,250 *Guaranteed Student Loan $ 2,500 *Perkins Loan $ 1,070 *College Grant $ 6,220

TOTAL AWARD: $11,040

Tanya D'Angelo

Tanya is one of five children from a family in Ohio. Dad is an attorney, and mom does not work outside the home. Along with an $80,000 annual income, the D'Angelos have an equity of about $90,000 in their home, approx. $25,000 in investments, and a $15,000 savings account. Tanya has decided to major in agriculture and life sciences. Her expenses look like this:

*Tuition, Room and Board, Books Personal Expenses, and Travel $15,350

-Less Tanya's Contribution $ 1,050 -Less Parent's Contribution $14,300

FINANCIAL NEED: $ 0

AWARD: $ 0

Jackie Byers

Jackie is from a family of three in New York City. She and her sister live with their widowed mother. Mrs. Byers' income consists of $10,500 in wages from her cashier job and $7,200 in social security benefits. Mrs. Byers is enrolled part-time at a local community college. Family assets are minimal. Jackie plans to major in industrial and labor relations. Her financial need stacks up like this:

*Tuition, Room and Board, Books, Personal Expenses and Travel $10,950

-Less Jackie's contribution $ 1,050 -Less Her Mother's contribution $ 400

FINANCIAL NEED: $ 9,500

As a result Jackie received the following financial aid package:

*College Work-Study $1,250 *Guaranteed Student Loan $1,900 *New York State Tap Award and

Regents College Scholarship $3,030 *Pell Grant $2,050 *College Grant $1,270

AWARD: $9,500

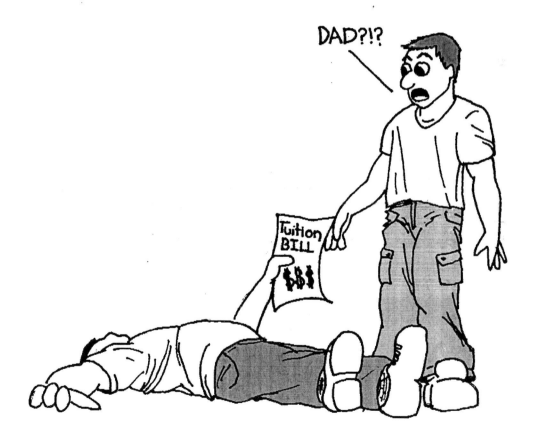

FINANCIAL PLANNING WORKSHEET

Before you apply for financial aid you must find out how much your total college expenses will be and the reasons for them. Use this form to calculate your expenses.

EXPENSES FOR FRESHMAN YEAR: Private   State U.   State School:

Tuition		
Room		
Board		
Books/Supplies		
Special Fees		
Traveling Expenses		
Clothing		
Spending Money		
Total Estimated Cost	A:	

FUNDS AVAILABLE TO YOU:

Parent's Contribution
Student's Savings Student's
Summer Job
Other Sources
Total Estimated Cash Available
FINANCIAL NEED A- B:

FINANCIAL AID RESOURCES

College Board Cost and Financial Aid 2005. College Board; 732 pp; $23.95. Explains components and procedures in an easy-to-understand manner, detailing the financial facts for over 3,000 colleges.

The College Board Scholarship Handbook 2004. College Board; 616 pp; $26.95. Contains valuable advice, with facts on over 2,000 scholarships, internships, and loans. Also included is a CD-ROM.

Directory of Financial Aids for Minorities, 1993-1995. Gail Ann Schlacter and R. David Weber. Reference Service Press, 1100 Industrial Road, Suite 9, San Carlos, CA 94070. (415) 594-0743; 515 pp; $45.00. Scholarship and fellowship groups include minorities, Asian-Americans, Hispanics, Native Americans, and African-Americans. The index categorizes entries by subject, geographic location, programs and calendar.

Directory of Financial Aids for Women, 2003-2005. Gail A. Schlacter and R. David Weber. Reference Service Press. 548 pp; $45.00.

Financial Aid: A Partial List of Resources for Women, fifth edition, 1990. Julie Kuhn Ehrhart. Association of American Colleges: 1818 R Street, N.W., Washington, DC 20009; (202) 387-3760. 20 pp; $3.50.

Financial Aid for Asian Americans, 2003-2005. Gail Ann Schlacter and R. David Weber, Reference Service Press. 328 pp; $37.50.

Financial Aid for Hispanic Americans, 2003-2005. Gail Ann Schlacter and R. David Weber, Reference Service Press. 465 pp; $40.00.

Financial Aid for the Disabled and their Families, 2004-2006. Gail Ann Schlacter and R. David Weber, Reference Service Press. 502 pp; $40.00.

Financial Aid for Veterans, Military Personnel, and Their Dependents, 2004-2006. Gail Ann Schlacter and R. David Weber, Reference Service Press. 417 pp; $40.00.

Money-winning Scholarship Interviews and Essays: Inside Strategies from Judges and Winners, 2002. Gen S. Tanabe and Kelly Y. Tanabe, SuperCollege: 4546 B10 El Camino Real, #281, Los Altos, CA 94022; (650) 618-2221. 256 pp; $17.95. Tips abound on acing interviews and essays, with numerous "winning" and "bad" essays as well as sample interview questions and answers.

Paying for College without Going Broke, 2004. Kalman A. Chany and Geoff Martz, Princeton Review. 352 pp; $20.00. Gives numerous strategies for keeping admission costs low.

The Scholarship Book: The Complete Guide to Private-Sector Scholarships, Fellowships, Grants, and Loans for Undergraduates, 2004. Daniel J. Cassidy and Ellen Schneid. Prentice Hall Press, One Lake St., Upper Saddle River, NJ ; (201) 236-7000. 630 pp; $30.00. A directory of more than 50,000 scholarships, grants, and internships, this book reveals how to assess and maximize one's skills and achievements.

Scholarships for African-American Students, 2003. Peterson's; 480 pp; $14.95.

Scholarships for Asian-American Students, 2003. Peterson's; 480 pp; $14.95.

Scholarships for Hispanic Students, 2003. Peterson's; 480 pp; $14.95.

Scholarships, Grants, and Prizes, 2004. Peterson's. 700 pp; $29.95. Covers more than 1.6 million awards from different organizations, and the necessary steps to apply for them.

The Scholarship Scouting Report: An Insider's Guide to America's Best Scholarships, 2003. Ben Kaplan, HarperResource. 384 pp; $21.95. This book helps students understand the ways of winning scholarships through interviews and personal reports.